WALK IN MY SHOES

WALK IN MY SHOES

By

PATRICK HAYES

Word of His Mouth Publishers
Mooresboro, NC

All Scripture quotations are taken from the **King James Version** of the Bible.

ISBN: 978-1-941039-46-5
Printed in the United States of America
©2024 Patrick Hayes

Word of His Mouth Publishers
Mooresboro, NC
www.wordofhismouth.com

Dedicated to my wife, Judy

...who has followed me from the days of Al Manning's pleading for bus drivers in Margate, Florida, to the days when God moved us from Ft. Lauderdale, Florida, to Hammond, Indiana – having two small children and expecting another – to see a Chicago winter for the first time.

Seven years later, she followed me to an unfamiliar city in Ohio, a state in which I had promised God that I would never live, to start Berean Baptist Church. She watched as God vindicated our ministry there, and then, after twelve years, she followed me again as God directed us to leave Ohio and move to North Carolina.

Still by my side after fifty-eight years of marriage, she is the one whom God has used to create many of the answers to prayer recorded in this book. I thank God for her patience with me.

I love you, Jude.

Bud

Isaiah 65:24

And it shall come to pass, that before they call, I will answer; and while they are yet speaking, I will hear.

My God tells me that I don't have to stand up in a large public meeting and tell others what I need. I can simply ask Him, and sometimes, according to Isaiah 65:24, He's already sending the answer even before I ask Him.

Walk in My Shoes tells many stories in which God met needs about which no one else knew. Often, my wife and I talked to each other and to God about these needs, and lo and behold! God provided! What do red drapes, police officers, and RV parking have to do with each other? Well, friend, they were all from God answering prayers.

This book of answered prayers has no extra drama, for who needs drama when God is involved? As Numbers 23:23 mentions, "What God hath wrought," please know that these stories are living proof that God means what He says in Matthew 6:33, "But seek ye first the kingdom of God, and His righteousness; and all these things [food, raiment, shelter] shall be added unto you." As you read, let your attention be drawn to the heart of God, Who longs to hear from you.

We thank the hundreds of laborers who have helped bring glory and honor to our Lord Jesus Christ from Ft Lauderdale to Syracuse, NY, down south to Austin, TX, and out west to Albuquerque, NM, through the restaurants on Veterans Day that God gave us to glorify Him.

4

Romans 11:36 *For of Him, and through Him, and to Him, are all things: to whom be glory for ever. Amen.*

Table of Contents

Chapter 1
My Youth

My story begins with my birth in 1949 in Florida. While growing up, I heard the names *Jesus* and *God* in all different situations. Dad's inability to deal with the various cultures of people he met while in the US Army before and during World War II led him to use the name of *Jesus* in anger often.

Mom was the opposite: a very religious Pentecostal, she never used His name in anger. Often at the church, cleaning or doing other work, Mom participated in almost anything the church offered.

Dad continued to ignore church and God until one day when I was fourteen years old. He came home and announced that his cancer would probably kill him in six months. During those six months, he went to a tent revival in Miami and walked the sawdust trail, not praying for salvation but hoping to receive healing. He never recovered from his illness even after he had visited the altar.

During this time, I sat under a very evangelistic style of preaching, in that, the pastor always encouraged his church members to hand out Gospel tracts. The church was full of emotional experiences that confused me. Once I started my own job and had my own car, I moved out of that type of church.

The Vietnam War was coming about the time of my high school graduation; my neighbor and many friends signed up to serve in the military. So, as a young eighteen-year-old mason tender working for $1.10 per hour, I visited the US Air Force recruiting office and soon found myself at Basic Training in Amarillo, Texas.

After Basic Training, I returned home and married Judy, my beautiful high school sweetheart. A year later, she was pregnant, and I received orders to go to Vietnam. Our son was three months old when I left.

Being in Vietnam in the Air Force was good for me. The work hours were long, and I learned responsibility very quickly. As maintenance personnel for jet aircrafts, I was responsible for maintaining the F-100 fighters before they returned to the flight line for their bombing missions.

After four years in the US Air Force in the early 70s, I took my discharge in Tampa, Florida. After a few years, we moved closer to our families in the Fort Lauderdale/Miami area.

Chapter 2
My Introduction to a Different Church

One day, while I was taking off my work boots, Joseph, our oldest son, came into the house after playing with the children from next door. He asked me a question I had never heard coming from a four-year-old: "Daddy, who is Jesus Christ?"

The neighbors had been talking to him about Jesus and trying to get him to go to church with them. Joseph's question brought up some other life-changing questions. Both Judy and I realized that our children needed to be in church, but they were not going with the neighbors; they were going with us. So we threw ourselves into church.

During this time, my wife shared with me one night that she really didn't like the flooring in our house. This conversation was one of our requests that God answered two years later in a very unusual way. We still talk about how God provided this need without our praying for it or speaking to others about it. The answer to this request, described later, was from only God.

While serving at Calvary Baptist Church in Ft. Lauderdale, we were introduced to the bus ministry. The church, having buses for its Christian school, decided to run the buses on Sunday to pick up children for Sunday school. With so much more running, these buses needed a maintenance man, and the Sunday bus ministry needed a director: Brother Al Manning was that man.

One Sunday morning, my wife and I were visiting with our adult Sunday School class, eating doughnuts and drinking coffee. Al Manning, a big man, stood in the doorway and announced, "Look at you people – sitting around drinking coffee and eating doughnuts while I have buses with no drivers. Can't anyone help me?"

My wife, Judy, poked me in the ribs and asked, "You drive a tractor-trailer for your mom; can't you drive a bus?" Thus began my bus ministry. Cal Rayburn, a student at Pillsbury Baptist College, was the bus captain while I drove a sixty-six-passenger bus. This man was truly my mentor in this new ministry.

Across America, many pastors were using buses to bring in children for church, and our pastor realized that he needed to hire a professional bus director with education and experience. Once this man organized our church bus ministry, we had twelve buses bringing three hundred to four hundred children to church every Sunday, causing every Saturday and Sunday to be busy workdays.

One idea from this new bus ministry director was "Candy Drop Day." He brought five thousand Milky Way bars and planned to drop them from a helicopter onto the Christian school's football field full of expectant children. But he failed to realize that five thousand candy bars and I couldn't fit in the helicopter at the same time, and, more importantly, he failed to realize that Fort Lauderdale temperature melts chocolate; therefore, when the day was over, chocolate was everywhere – on the football field, on the children, in the bus – everywhere!

Another idea that I had, that I had read about in a bus promotional book, brought more memorable results. Children who were to chase a greased pig were sorely disappointed when the pig wouldn't run. The poor little pig just sat trembling in fear in the middle of the football field.

Oh, yes, we learned quite a bit during those three years. The pastor of Calvary Baptist Church learned that educated and experienced men sometimes do not make good bus ministry leaders, so he asked me to be the bus ministry director and to lead the senior citizen ministry. I was busy for the Lord.

Chapter 3
God's Providence

After serving for three years at Calvary Baptist Church in Ft. Lauderdale, we moved to West Palm Beach for a year while preparing to go to Bible college in Hammond, Indiana. Almost at the end of this year, my wife and I came to the understanding that our God had been listening to our conversations at night. I encourage the reader to be careful with your thoughts because God is listening!

Part of my preparation to go to college was to find housing for my family, which now included two children and one on the way. I drove back and forth from West Palm Beach, Florida, and Hammond, Indiana, looking for housing and a job that would allow me to attend school during the day. One day, I happened upon the Meadows Apartment complex. The receptionist made it very clear that their apartments were full; no one was moving out anytime soon. She encouraged me to check back in a week or so. I didn't want to drive all the way back to West Palm Beach without securing lodging for my family, so I stayed for a week with some friends as I began to look for a job.

I had visited a steel company a few times during my previous job searches, but each time, there were thirty or forty people standing in line to fill out an application. The Lord encouraged me to go back to this factory, so I did. There was absolutely no line, and the business manager was in his office. While speaking with him, he showed me the stack of applications sitting on his desk, the applications he had to go through to hire someone before he left for his week-long vacation that very day. During our conversation, the manager's boss reported to him that another worker had just quit and that he, the business manager, needed to replace him before he could leave for vacation.

The business manager turned to me and asked, "Ya want a job?"

Needless to say, God had this situation worked out completely to His glory. The manager immediately showed me the machine floor where all the steel presses were working. He walked me to a twelve-foot-tall cutting press and said, "We could hire monkeys to do this job, but if you want it, you can have it." I was hired and God began to show me the way that He moves.

Now that I had a job, I returned to the Meadows Apartment complex. While I was trying to do my part, God was doing His part behind the scenes. The receptionist told me that their board of directors had voted just that morning to allow the model apartment to be leased. She told me the dimensions of the apartment, held the key out to me, and asked if I wanted to see the apartment. Well, yes, of course, I wanted to see what God had provided for my family and me!

As I opened the door, I immediately remembered a conversation that my wife and I had two years prior about the floor in our home. She wanted a bedroom with white carpets, a red bedspread, and red drapes to match. I was standing in the exact décor that Judy wanted – God had provided! The receptionist was uncertain as to the reason that I was thrilled to have that particular apartment; I couldn't wait to get home and tell Judy what God had done!

But I didn't tell Judy about the décor in the apartment – I just went back to West Palm Beach, packed up our household, and returned to Indiana. When Judy saw our new apartment, she, too, remembered the conversation two years prior. What a time we had discussing that God had worked in the smallest details: a job, the board of directors' decision to rent the model apartment (one that no one had ever lived in), and the exact design that Judy had requested years prior. What a great God we serve!

Chapter 4
Unexpected Conviction

Those seven years in Hammond, Indiana, (five as a student, two working to pay off the school bill) were exciting days: many prayers were answered that will never be forgotten. The most exciting day was the day when I acknowledged that I was not saved.

Friday night, February 22, 1980, as I was helping Sherwood Thorton, my co-worker, close down the machine shop at Pulman Standard, I was very convicted about encouraging Sherwood to come to church with me on Sunday. Sherwood was the head machine inspector, and I was one of many press operators. The more I tried to talk with Sherwood about going to church, the more he made excuses about why he could not come. Finally, he looked up at me from his desk, pointed a finger at me, and asked, "What makes you so sure you're going to Heaven?"

The Bible answer fell out of my mouth – after all, I had led many folks to the Lord, brought folks to church, and knew the answer, but I was troubled. As I punched out for the night, tremendous conviction overwhelmed me that I had just lied to Sherwood about my going to Heaven. The conviction did not let up even into that very restless night.

Saturday morning, I attended the Fisherman's Club at Obie's Restaurant. About 120 men always gathered, ate breakfast, and listened to a sermon to encourage us in witnessing about Christ. That day, God had that sermon planned in advance for me. George

Godfrey, the speaker, used Bible verses to teach about preachers who were lost – very sincere guys who had never been born again. While I listened, conviction about my lost condition dogged me.

Chapter 5
Coming to Christ

As I sat in that Fisherman's Club meeting, thinking about my salvation, I started remembering the "good moral decisions" that I had made in my past that made me believe that I was born again. Here are a few of those decisions.

Before we married, Judy and I were watching a movie at a drive-in theater in my '54 Plymouth sedan. One actor used the names *Jesus Christ* and *God* a number of times. Finally, I looked at Judy and told her that I had heard enough of that language. We left the theater and never went back.

One time after we married, we were sitting on Haulover Beach in Miami with our two boys. A woman came walking down the beach in the typical beach attire. As I noticed her severe immodesty, I realized that this was not a good situation for me or our boys to see. I looked at my wife and asked her to pick up the blanket and radio while I picked up the cooler. Joseph and Lance, our boys, clueless as to the reason, followed us off the beach; we never returned.

I also remember the effects that liquor had on me while I was in Vietnam. When I returned stateside, I brought liquor into my home and shared it with Judy. One night, both of us made another one of those good moral decisions: I poured all that liquor and beer down the drain, and we've never drunk again.

Once, I was out visiting for our Sunday School class in Ft. Lauderdale while being mentored by a very wealthy real estate salesman in the church. While we were out, the topic of strong drink came up. He told me that he had a contract on a piece of property that was going to be used for a liquor store. While he talked about his profit, I expressed to him my belief in the evil of the liquor industry and the cigarette industry. The car ride back to the church was very quiet. I certainly had an understanding of the liquor industry and the cigarette industry. Smoking one cigarette in my life was enough to make me turn away from it.

Another day, God prompted my heart in another situation. It was Sunday, and after coming home from church, I was relaxed on my couch, watching what the cameraman thought was pretty attractive – the Dallas Cowboys cheerleaders in their scant clothing and provocative body movements. The more I saw of those girls and their behavior, the more I knew how wrong it was to allow that kind of behavior in my home. Holy Spirit conviction made me turn off that television, and the television was sold that week. Yes, more "good moral decisions."

Maybe the ultimate "good moral decision" was made when I decided to sell our newly purchased home and move my wife and children from Ft. Lauderdale, Florida, to Hammond, Indiana, to attend Bible college. Surely, God was pleased with my actions. Yes, He was, but they weren't enough to save me from Hell.

So, as I was sitting in the Fisherman's Club, listening to Brother Godfrey that Saturday morning, I was under severe conviction about the words *born again* and Nicodemus being a *morally good* man. Yet Jesus made it clear to him in John 3:3 that being morally good is not enough when He said, "Verily, verily, I say unto thee, except a man be born again, he cannot see the kingdom of God." I kept remembering all these events in my life where I was trying to please God with "good moral decisions," like speaking against alcohol, like standing against immodest apparel in my home, like my dumping all the alcohol in my house down the drain. Yet they were not what being *born again* was all about. Good moral decisions will not take a man to Heaven.

During my seven years in Hammond, the most exciting time was when I realized that God had stopped what He was doing on February 22, 1980, and had Sherwood Thornton point his finger at me and demand, "What makes you so sure you're going to Heaven?" Then, just twelve hours later, a preacher preached a sermon about preachers who had never been born again.

My realization that God was visiting me, drawing me to Himself, and showing me that I needed salvation was a great moment. That Saturday, I admitted that I was lost. Yet I still drove to Chicago, going through all the motions of a Saturday soul winner. I finally realized the truth of 1 Peter 1:18-19 that "ye were not redeemed with corruptible things, as silver and gold, from your vain conversation received by tradition from your fathers; But with the precious blood of Christ, as of a lamb without blemish and without spot."

The next morning, Sunday, I called the preacher at 7:30 a.m. and said, "Sir, I have a problem with your preaching from yesterday."

21

Brother Godfrey said, "You're lost, and you have a decision to make."

That Sunday, February 24, 1980, was the greatest day of my life when Jesus saved a pretty religious man. He showed me that all the things I had done were fine, but they did not earn me salvation. My eyes were opened to my "vain conversation," and I asked Jesus to forgive my sin and be my Savior.

From February 24, 1980, until my graduation from college, my family experienced many answers to prayer, from college bills needing to be paid, to our children's school bills needing to be paid, to having more children (April, David, and Joy, and two who went to Heaven). God was good to us!

Chapter 6
An Encounter with the Policeman

During the five years of college and working night shifts at the factories, both my wife and I learned valuable lessons in prayer while learning to have God's attention and His presence in our lives. One night after working at the factory, exhaustion had probably impacted my thinking. I arrived home at the Meadows Apartment complex around 11:30 p.m. The parking lot was about a hundred yards from our apartment, and as I was walking down the sidewalk to get to our apartment, the sidewalk lit up behind me. When I looked back, I saw that a car had driven over the curb and was driving toward me on the sidewalk. Instead of stopping to see what was about to happen, I started running for safety in my apartment. Unknown to me, another officer had parked his car and had run ahead to meet me at the end of the sidewalk. By the time I reached my door, the car on the sidewalk had caught up with me, and the other policeman was standing in front of me with his gun pulled, waiting for me. What an experience!

The officer explained that there had been a convenience store robbery in the area that night, and the robber had been driving the same type of car as I was driving. The officer gave me a long lecture about the importance of not running when being chased by a police car, something that I normally wouldn't have done if I had not been so exhausted. That night our God was truly answering a prayer for safety that had not even been expressed.

Chapter 7
My Failing Body

At Hyles-Anderson College, every student, no matter the major, had to have so many hours of serving in the bus ministry during the school year in order to graduate. In my senior year, I realized that I didn't have enough hours (credits) of bus ministry to graduate on time. I had been working my normal job at the factory, taking the normal class load, working both the Saturday and Sunday bus programs, and trying to manage my home. I was working seven days a week in school, in the factory, and in the church. One morning in class, my Bible teacher, Les Smith, said words that no student wants to hear from the teacher, "Patrick, I would like to see you after class." After class, Mr. Smith said, "Patrick, you're turning yellow." I knew that I was sick and tired from the schedule, but no one else had told me. Les Smith didn't know it, but my bowels had stopped working for about a month, and I was losing weight. During this sickness, we learned more about prayer.

After a visit to the University of Chicago medical clinic that worked with colon and bowel disorders, I was still having problems with no answers. We tried a local health food doctor who understood colon disorders. After much prayer, this doctor advised us to visit Lewis Shelton, a local colon specialist. It had been eight weeks with no bowel movements, and I was still trying to work and attend classes.

This colon specialist was also the foreman of the maintenance department of a local steel factory. How he managed to sustain both of these different occupations, I'll never know! His thorough knowledge of the colon and of prayer was used by God to save my life. This man, who believed in prayer, helped folks with bowel disorders from his home. After I met with Lewis Shelton and used colon irrigation, my bowels began to move. When this started to happen, both of us were praising God for such an answer to prayer. After a few weeks of a change in diet and some changes in my schedule, God touched my body, and it began to function properly. Once I was able to accumulate the proper credits in the bus ministry, I was ready for graduation. Sometimes, God just sends an answer, and sometimes, God sends a human to answer the prayer request. He knows what is best.

Chapter 8
God Listens to Prayers About Shoes

During my college days, my wife, Judy, did babysitting jobs to help bring in some income. She had been setting aside some money, planning to buy me some new shoes for college graduation. Because money was so tight, there were no visits to local shoe stores to buy shoes on a whim, so we really didn't know how much shoes cost. Somehow, though, it seemed that our shoes didn't need to be replaced, for our Heavenly Father knew just what we needed and when we needed it.

Judy found some men's shoe stores in the area, and one day, we went shoe shopping at the Sears River Oaks Mall outside of Chicago. Boy, were we ever surprised at the high cost of decent shoes! I definitely didn't want her to spend all her savings on a pair of brand-new shoes for me. Both of us were discouraged and wanted to go home. At the last store we walked by, a Florsheim shoe store, I stopped to just wish for a pair. Judy said, "Let's just go home. You're not going to spend that kind of money for a pair of shoes."

She was right. But as I stood at the store display, I pointed to a rather expensive pair of brown Florsheim Imperial shoes, and I prayed, "Lord, if I had that much money, I wouldn't spend it on those shoes, but I sure would like to have a pair of them." I turned away from the window and drove home with no new shoes. Graduation was right around the corner, and God had a plan.

26

Judy had been serving in the church nursery for a few years with a lady named Ruth, who was much older than my wife. Ruth and her husband, Ken, were both very active pillars in the church, he being a deacon. Ken had recently passed away, and the week of graduation, Ruth called Judy to explain that the family wanted to clean out his closet and asked if I'd be willing to come by the house to see if any items would fit me before they took the clothes to the mission. Oh, what an interesting time this was – God was planning to do something that only He, in His love, could do.

Judy and I went to her house as soon as possible. When we arrived at her luxurious house, we saw that Ruth's son had laid out some very well-made, expensive suits on the pool table for me to try on. While we chatted about the clothes, Ruth turned to her son and said, "Go up to your dad's shoe press and bring down his shoes. Let's see if they might fit Brother Patrick."

He came down the stairs with a grocery bag and a handful of shoes. He set a chair down and asked me to sit and start trying on the shoes. When I tried on the first pair, they fit. Instantly, I remembered the hours just a week earlier that Judy and I had spent looking for a pair of shoes for graduation with no success. Ruth knew that we had been looking for shoes, but she did not know that I had told God which exact pair I really wanted.

When Ruth's son was filling the bag with shoes, he had taken a brand-new pair, purchased just a few weeks earlier, and placed them first in the bag. Now, they were the last to be taken out. As I pulled out the last pair of shoes, I noticed they were... yes, you guessed it...

brown Florsheim Imperial shoes! The exact shoes that I had told the Lord that I wanted! As I began to tell Ruth and her son the story behind the shoes, Ruth told us that Ken had just bought the shoes and had never worn them outside, he only wore them inside the house to "break the in."

God knew about our trip to the Sears River Oaks Mall. He knew about all the different stores we had visited. He heard my conversation with Him while standing in front of the Florsheim display window. He used my wife's faithfulness in the church nursery to meet a need that was spoken to no one. When I told this story to a pastor in Ohio, he replied, "I've never had anything like that ever happen for me." To each of my readers, please take time to talk with the Lord and express your needs and wants. He is listening! All we were looking for was one pair of shoes, and yet, God blessed me with not only the exact pair I wanted but a whole bag of shoes!

Chapter 9
All on the Altar

After this exciting answer to my request for the shoes, it was two years before we were able to leave Hammond, Indiana, to start Berean Baptist Church. During these two years, since we didn't have the money or a destination, I was living a normal life with my wife and children, and thus, I had time to give much thought as to the reason that I had sold my home in Ft. Lauderdale and had moved all the way to Hammond to go to Bible college. The time out of school allowed me to create a small part-time job mowing yards, a job which led me to meet Bill, a small lawnmower shop owner. God later used him to answer a prayer.

In my second year after finishing college, I became very concerned about what we were going to do as a family for the Lord. While I examined my life, the Lord brought Danny Woodward into my life at the factory. We seldom saw each other, but this particular night, our paths crossed. He then asked me a life-changing question: "Patrick, have you ever gone to the altar to tell the Lord that you would do anything He showed you or led you to do?" I pondered this idea. I had been out of school for two years, and my school bills were caught up – there was no logical reason for us to stay in Hammond.

Right after my college graduation, a deacon in the church promised me that he would pay my moving expenses to wherever God led us to start a church. I was confident that he was very sincere. With his promise and

Danny Woodwards' counseling about "tell God you would do anything," it was time to visit the altar at church. I went to the altar and told the Lord, "Please use me. I am willing to go anywhere." Nobody knew why I went to the altar; no one knew about the prayer.

The next week, I received a phone call from the ministry placement office at the college. This office had never called me during these two years, nor had I given them my name or told them that I was looking for a ministry. It seems that an evangelist, Larry Clayton, had called the school to look for a man to start a church. He contacted me and invited me to Cambridge, Ohio, where the Cleveland Baptist Church had started a church.

When I heard *Ohio*, memories from my Vietnam days flooded back. I had worked with some folks from Ohio, and for some unknown reason, I had not gotten along with them very well. I promised God that I'd never live in Ohio if He were to get me out of Vietnam alive. It's rather interesting how God has a way of teaching His children!

Once we arrived in Cambridge, Ohio, Larry Clayton gave me a tour of the entire county, trying to convince me that the city needed a Baptist church. Remembering my promise to the Lord about going anywhere He led me, I was having trouble making a decision about moving to Cambridge. When I arrived back in Hammond, I called Larry Clayton and told him that I had no peace about moving to Cambridge. Disappointed, he wanted God's man there to have peace.

The very next week, I asked my family to go on a vacation to visit relatives in Miami so that I could be alone to fast and pray about Cambridge and my promise to the Lord at the altar. I was on the third day of my fast, praying for God's will, when I received a letter from a seminar administration. During this waiting time, after telling the Lord that I'd go anywhere, I registered to go to a seminar in Chicago held for pastors. Convinced that I was starting a church, I thought I qualified to attend the seminar. The seminar administration thought otherwise and sent the denial letter.

I called the seminar's main office to understand the reason for their denying my application. I told the receptionist that I had just returned from Cambridge, Ohio, where we were praying about starting a church. As soon as I said, "Cambridge, Ohio," I heard her say, "Oh, my aunt lives in Cambridge, and when we go visit her, there is no church to attend in Cambridge. It is the most desolate city."

Here I was on the third day of fasting, trying to get peace about moving to Cambridge, Ohio, and this lady in Chicago, who knows nothing of my situation, told me that Cambridge was the most desolate city in America for churches. God doesn't talk to His children verbally out loud, but that day, God *did* talk to me. After this conversation, I called Evangelist Clayton to see if he had found a pastor for Cambridge. He had not. I thought that we would soon be on the way to Cambridge, Ohio.

Once we made the commitment to move, knowing that I had been promised financial help from the deacon two years prior, I gave my two-week notice at the factory. I then made the appointment with the deacon. This eye-opening meeting tested my faith. This deacon made it clear to me that he had been praying about fulfilling his promise, and he believed that if God were in the picture, then God would provide the finances to make the move. Going to work for the next two weeks with five children and a wife to feed and knowing that I had already given my notice at the factory was quite difficult. My close co-workers knew that I was moving.

On Monday morning, the day after the deacon reneged on his promise of financial help, Ken, a fellow worker, told me that he'd like to talk with me at lunch. Ken, who worked in the tool crib, always stayed to himself, not saying much to me about anything, now wanted to talk to me at lunch. Not a churchgoer, he was not interested in anything spiritual.

During our lunch break, Ken expressed to me that he appreciated all the time we had worked together. Then he stunned me with these exact words: "Patrick, give some thought to it, and I will write you a check tonight at the end of the shift for whatever amount of money you think you need to move."

Have you ever felt the hand of God move on you? Here, this quiet, long-haired, earring-wearing, unchurched man, out of the blue, said, "I will write you a check for whatever amount of money you think you need." When the shift ended that night, Ken came to me with his checkbook in hand and fulfilled his promise by writing me a check. The deacon was still my friend, but I quickly learned about Jesus taking care of my needs, and I needed no other source.

Chapter 10
Desolate Ohio

Once we had moved into the house that the church in Cleveland, Ohio, had provided for us, we started meeting the neighbors. We soon realized that the Independent Baptists had been coming to Cambridge since the 40s, trying to start a church. Between the early 40s and the mid-80s, when God moved us there, I was the seventh or eighth pastor who had tried to start a church in the city. Previously, my wife and I had started bus routes and junior church for bus riders, but now we stepped into an area of Christianity that became a real eye-opener.

For the next twelve years, the Hayes family was taught many valuable lessons about life and about God. I had no doubt that God wanted me in Cambridge and He wanted the people there to have a Bible-believing church. I was thirty-five years old with a wife and five children, starting our first church in a city that had three Presbyterian churches in downtown Cambridge – all within rock-throwing distance of each other. The receptionist in Chicago was correct when she told me that Cambridge was desolate of churches – Gospel-preaching churches!

It wasn't long before we discovered that Cambridge was one of the major headquarters for the Ohio Masonic Temple. Then we discovered that our mayor had been arrested in Cleveland for wearing women's clothing, yet, at the next election, he was re-elected!

Since we had no families to start our church, I decided to lay out a map of the city and begin a door-to-door program inviting folks to the new Baptist church in Cambridge. We started with our neighbor. I introduced myself and my oldest son, Joseph, to the lady next door. As soon as I used the word *church* and explained what we were doing, the lady asked, "Have you been downtown yet?" The answer was simple, but she didn't give me a chance to answer her. She opened the screen door a little wider and said, "Sir, we have enough churches; we do not need any more," and closed the door.

So we went to the neighbor on the other side of our house. This neighbor lady came out on the porch, and we began a homey-type conversation. Once the conversation turned to *Heaven* and the *Gospel*, the lady said, "The way you've described Heaven… I'm having too much fun here to go to such a place like that," then she walked back into the house.

After these two visits, I realized that God had built our faith in Hammond to prepare us to start a Bible-believing church in Cambridge.

After much prayer, we felt we should rent the conference room at the Days Inn in Cambridge for a service. We then printed a few thousand brochures and handed them out door-to-door. When the day arrived to have our first meeting, I realized that I had coffee and donuts for the meeting, but I had forgotten something very important – to pay the rent for the conference room. People were coming into the room (some were Christians from other cities to encourage folks to come), but I was out of money.

When I humbled myself and admitted to the desk clerk the trouble I was in, he said, "Sir, someone came through here today and paid the rent for your new church to start."

All the faith-building events in Hammond and all the uninterested people here taught me that God was still interested in Cambridge. It was not long before we started Wednesday night prayer meetings.

Chapter 11
Church Troubles and Blessings

After a few months with Sunday and Wednesday night services, we were introduced to another church in the area that was interested in merging our two congregations together to make a stronger, unified church. This proposed merger was the first major decision of the Cambridge ministry, and I made a mess of it! My church, composed of new converts, merged with a congregation who had been in their building for many years, a congregation definitely set in their ways. The Lord allowed the merger which, in time, allowed much heartache for the next eleven years.

The church with whom we merged was not ready to hear a new style of preaching or to change their already established standards. Sometimes, merging churches is smooth, and other times, it is not. Through the daily and weekly upheavals in ministry, God still gave me a reminder that He always knows what's going on in our lives and that He always answers prayers in His time and on time. Here's the story:

I had been taught by two pastor friends, one of whom was a missionary with a large mission organization, that every pastor needs to go visit a mission field sometime in their ministry. Both of them had visited the field several times. I saw the need for me to do this and suggested that they pay for my way. That suggestion did not go over well, but eventually, they agreed to pay half. I needed $500 – they would pay $250, and I'd find the other $250. I definitely didn't have the money to ride in a Silver Eagle coach to Mexico and stay for a week. Since both my wife and I agreed that visiting the mission field would help me as a pastor, we started praying for the money, knowing that it would have to come in a very unusual way.

Time was running out to have the money for the trip. One week before the money was due, I received a phone call from Bill, the lawn mower business owner in Hammond, Indiana, with whom I had been only casual friends in my lawn mowing business. It took me a few minutes to remember him. In this call, he told me that he was driving to West Virginia and had stopped in New Concord, a city next to Cambridge. He asked, "Patrick, do you still have a church in Cambridge? We haven't seen you for years and would like to see your church building."

Bill and his wife walked through our building just making small talk, and I invited them to stay for a meal but they declined. After they got back into the truck to leave, Bill handed me a roll of money. As they drove down the road, I looked in my hand – five $50 bills! This was the $250 for the mission trip.

I immediately began to think about groceries and other bills that could be paid, but the more plans I made for that $250, the more I remembered the thought that we knew that the $250 for the mission trip would be coming in an unusual way. The plan for groceries went away as I pondered the unusual way that God provided this money; a man and his wife drove all the way from Hammond, passing through our neighborhood to West Virginia to visit friends, stopping to see a fellow who

37

used to buy lawn mower parts from him, not staying for a meal, but just handing over $250 at a time I needed it. I called the mission director to tell him that I had the money and would send it to him for my trip.

I went on the trip and would highly recommend that a pastor visit the mission field. God certainly must have thought it was important enough to set up all these circumstances. Amen!

Chapter 12
Unrepentant Sinners and Sadness

Prayers, like the one about the mission trip money provided by the lawn-mower repair man Bill, assured us that God was still taking note of what was going on in Cambridge. However, more trouble started, as is common in any church.

The church was growing enough that we started Sunday school classes and door-knocking as part of evangelism. Because our church members were representing Jesus, I desired that they look different from the world and thus, I taught about dress standards in a Sunday morning service. That evening, two ladies, a mother and daughter, came to church wearing bib overalls. They very proudly presented themselves to me right before the service and asked, "Whatcha think about this?"

With their attitudes toward the preaching of God's Word, I knew that they would not be involved as Sunday school teachers. Both ladies had given testimony of their salvation, but I was very disappointed knowing that they weren't interested in the dress standards of our church. As time moved forward, these ladies, along with other family members, found more difficulty with the preaching of God's Word.

The following Sunday, the mother's twenty-one-year-old son showed his displeasure at the preaching of God's Word by showing me certain vulgar hand signals while I preached. While this showing of unrepentant attitude was occurring, another lady who had been coming to church for about a year, had attended Bible studies, and had invited us to her home to talk more about the Lord, came forward and accepted Christ as her Savior. Even while Satan was trying to disrupt the church, God was still harvesting souls!

The following Sunday, I was called at 4:00 a.m. by the local hospital morgue to identify a body that the Highway Patrol had brought into the morgue. Coming down the hallway of the hospital, all I could hear was the cries of distressed people. When I opened the room's door, I met the mother who had challenged me on the topic of modest apparel; now her son, who had been giving me derogatory hand signals while I was preaching, was dead, wrapped up in a body bag, the victim of a tragic speeding accident.

I was definitely learning about the fear of God and about prayer.

Chapter 13
Another Chance at Life

Our youngest son David had talked about joining the Marine Corps, and one particular day, he proved that he had some Marine in him.

I had just returned from a trip during which a church member and I had driven from Cambridge, Ohio, to Pensacola, Florida, picked up 100,000 John and Romans booklets, carried them to Chicago to be shipped to a missionary friend in Africa, and then returned to Cambridge all in two days. Neither of us realized how tired we were.

The following afternoon, I went to pick up my children from school. It was about a forty-five-minute drive to the school. I was not feeling well at all. The travels from the few days before and my current health issues at the time of colitis were seemingly creating an extreme health crisis that day for me. When the children got in the car, my daughter April immediately knew I was not okay. She offered to drive since she was a newly permitted driver, but I still felt a little uncomfortable for her to drive that far back home. So, I decided to stay behind the wheel and drive my family back home. Soon, that decision would prove that I was wrong in not allowing her to drive that day but, at the same time, show that the prayers that we prayed before leaving that school parking lot would be heard and answered in the most amazing and incredible way.

As I drove onto the highway, I could tell I was not okay. I remember telling the children to pray that we would make it home. In hindsight, I should have pulled over and allowed our new permitted driver to get a little more experience and drive us the rest of the way home.

We were one mile away from home when I remember blacking out. I was told that when that happened, my foot pressed into the gas peddle, making us go even faster. When I woke up, we were in mid-air, upside down, going over one of those famous Ohio hills. All I could say in that very horrific moment was, "God, please help my kids!" God saved my family that day!

The next thing I remember was April screaming, "Daddy, are you alive? Are you okay?" When I turned my head to look at her, I remember telling her to go get help. And then I blacked out and remember the next face being a person trying to figure out how they would get me out from under the steering wheel. The car was upside down, and water flowed through it from the creek bed where God had laid our car down. The Jaws of Life had been called after my children had gotten out of the car then somehow were able to make it up that huge hill and get help. April ran one way, and David ran the other, while Joy stayed with me. David proved that day that the call on his life to become a Marine was legitimate. While having a punctured lung and other severe issues from what just happened, he ran up the mountainous road towards our home to get his mother. God sent an individual who picked him up, brought him back to me, and then went and got Judy.

By the time Judy got to me and the children, Joy had made it up the hill, April had gotten more help, and the ambulances had arrived. Judy was the strongest I had known her to be. At that moment, she saw her children lying on the side of the road, bloodied, struggling to breathe, and having a hard time walking, being helped by the first responders. I heard her say to the Jaws of Life people who were with me, "Is my husband alive and okay?"

They loaded our children up in ambulances and took them away. Judy stayed and waited until they cut me out of our car, and she went with me in the ambulance to the hospital.

That day was a turning point in all of our lives. Jaws of Life told us later that night in the Emergency Room that they had seen hundreds of accidents just like ours, and people never walked away alive like we did. We were told my daughter April, who was sitting in the front seat, should have never survived that type of flip-and-roll accident. Usually, in those kinds of accidents, they said, the person in the passenger seat gets thrown out the window, and the car rolls over them, and they never survive.

Many thoughts go through my mind when I think about that day. But God had a plan in it all and gave me and my children another chance at life. Living for Him is what I have desired for me and my children. I pray daily that we all will fulfill the plan He has for us and that we never forget the hand of God and the angles who laid that car down in that cold creek bed that fateful day.

Chapter 14
The Mission Field of North Carolina

A missionary from overseas had come home from his field and started attending the church in Cambridge. This certainly looked like a blessing. He, along with his wife and six children, would be a great help to our church. However, it was just a few months into his time in Cambridge that the missionary felt the need to start visiting some of our church members, and I soon discovered that he felt that he needed to start a church in Cambridge... with church members whom he had misled about our church.

Troubles of this nature and family problems led us to resign from the church and move our family to Lattimore, North Carolina. At the age of forty-eight, thinking God was finished with me, I found a job in a food processing plant until I received a job at the local Pittsburgh Paint and Glass (PPG) factory. I needed the work and had no idea that 9/11 was coming to America. God had a place ready for me to serve Him.

PPG was an excellent learning experience for me. On the first day, all new employees had to take a tour of the plant. The tour guide knew that I had pastored a church in Ohio so he introduced me to people in the different areas of the factory as "a preacher coming to work for us from Ohio." The introduction did not help me make friends; I soon realized that a recent drug raid had occurred in the plant, and supposedly, the undercover officers were from Ohio.

Here I was – starting all over again at the age of forty-eight, with no one in the factory really understanding the last twelve years and the events that had taken place with my family. I no longer had a church office in which to study. This was a new normal for us.

The schedule was this: I worked two days from 8:00 a.m. to 8:00 p.m., and then I would rotate and work two night shifts. I was happy to have a job with a guaranteed salary and paycheck at the end of the week.

Here in the South, I learned about Baptist deacons who chewed tobacco and were exceptionally friendly with women who were not their wives. One Baptist deacon clarified to me that we needed to leave the "church talk" at home with the Gospel tracts.

PPG was a real mission field where, at the beginning of my time there, I had the liberty to leave Gospel literature where folks could read about the love of God. Soon, however, I saw the TV monitors in the breakroom announcing that there would be no religious articles of any nature left in the breakroom. Yet, as I will later explain, God still used unsaved workers there who helped the ministry.

Chapter 15
9/11 and the Birth of a New Ministry

When the 9/11 events took place here in America, God had me exactly where He wanted me. I was making a nice paycheck, but I was also killing myself with all the overtime hours.

The night of September 10, 2001, I had worked a midnight twelve-hour shift and was just getting off work the morning of 9/11 when the attacks began. I watched the events of the day as they took place – just like most Americans. When my wife came home from her job, I promised her and my Heavenly Father that I would do whatever God would lead me to do to take advantage of the situation to spread the Gospel to the American people. I had already been to the altar in my second year after college at Danny Woodward's urging to tell God that I would do anything He wanted me to do. I had no idea that He had already set a plan in motion to place the Gospel message in the hands of thousands of our troops.

The next day, September 12, while in Shelby, North Carolina, I saw lines of young people at the Armed Forced recruiting offices. The more I thought of these young people and the tasks ahead of them, the more I became burdened about giving them the Gospel. God used the images of those long lines of young people to steer me toward Ft. Bragg, North Carolina.

On October 1, I had three days off from work. I believed that I should go to Ft. Bragg Army base and see what God was going to do – a good idea but a small disaster nonetheless.

47

I left Shelby at 3:00 a.m. and headed for Ft. Bragg, 225 miles away. I had plenty of time to talk with the Lord and allow the Holy Spirit to remind me of times when my family visited downtown Miami, where, back in the 50s and 60s, it was very common for young people and even grown men to sell newspapers in the streets. For some reason, I couldn't shake the idea of selling newspapers in the street.

Once I arrived at one of the base gates, the waiting line to get on base was hours long. All vehicles were inspected with all doors, the hood, and the trunk open. Guards rolled underneath each car to inspect. Once I was able to get into the base, I realized why God was reminding me about those newspaper boys on the streets of Miami.

I had some John and Romans booklets with me, and I had placed Gospel tracts inside. I started giving them to any army soldier who would talk to me inside the base. Soon, an MP saw me sharing material and quickly directed my path to the chaplain's office to get approval to share my booklets with the troops. Here, I received a wake-up call from the Lord.

The Lt. Col. Army chaplain read me the riot act about the distribution of religious literature on the base and quickly informed me that if I continued, I would be taken to the brig. I began to listen to the Lord, Who was reminding me, again, about the newspaper boys on the street. He had an amazing mission planned for me.

The front gate of Ft. Bragg was actually quite dangerous: traffic entering the fort was controlled by only a traffic light and a yellow line separating the two lanes of traffic. During the ninety-second red light, I walked along the yellow line, approached the soldiers in their car, and handed them Gospel literature. It was a form of evangelism that only God could create.

Never, when I was in the Air Force or even when I was in Vietnam, did I have any idea that God would use my military time to be profitable for Him in these post-9/11 events. Once I realized that the streets were a very productive way to get the Gospel into the hands of soldiers, I began to make regular visits to the streets. I discovered that my wearing a Vietnam hat or shirt grabbed a soldier's attention quite quickly. My time in Vietnam fifty years ago now opened the door for me to share my testimony with the soldiers, and thus, most took the Gospel literature. My life was filled with working four twelve-hour days at PPG and then taking my three days off to travel to Ft. Bragg.

I soon realized that I needed help from my church. Previously, I had worked overtime to pay for my trips to Ft. Bragg and for the tracts and John and Romans booklets, but I had been spending my spare time traveling to the base instead of working overtime. When I approached my pastor about my ministry with the troops and about the financial needs for materials, his response was underwhelming: the church would not be able to help financially with the Gospel literature. Great disappointment set in.

As we continued the street work in 2002, I noticed a problem: when we handed the John and Romans literature with a Gospel tract to the soldier, the tract often fell out into the car floorboard when the soldier opened the literature. After many months of praying for a solution, I visited a church in Texas. When I entered, a greeter handed me a packet-type folder that held church literature for visitors. This same packet, or jacket, would very nicely hold the material that I was passing out at the military bases. Immediately, the Lord showed me that this was my prayer answered that no one knew about.

Once back home, the Lord encouraged me to create a military design for the jacket that would hold the material. This jacket was one of those answers to prayers that God used to show me Who was in charge of the mission.

Our son, David, had joined the Marine Corps before 9/11, and when God had me start the street work, he was already in training to go to Iraq. The year that the jacket was designed was the same year that he was stationed in Iraq. At this time, David had shipped to Iraq, and I had started making mission trips to Parris Island Marine Corps Base and Hunter Army Airfield in Savannah. We had always included John and Romans in the care packages that we sent to him, but we didn't know that David had been sharing the Gospel tracts and the John and Romans with some of his buddies.

God honored me with a major answer to prayer like only God does. I found a man who designed the front of the jackets to hold the tracts for the street work. I ordered five thousand jackets with the hope that I would have plenty of overtime work to pay for the material; however, the overtime work dwindled. The jackets were due to be picked up in just a few more weeks. The Lord was so merciful. The week that the printing company called me to pick up the jackets, I received a one-page letter from my son's then-gunnery sergeant from Iraq. Sent to Iraq in 2003, my youngest son, David, had shared some Gospel literature with his buddies on the ship. His gunnery sergeant expressed on pocket-size spiral notebook paper that "your son is doing a good job. I've not tithed for a long time, and I like what you're doing." His tithe check was $2,200, and my printing bill was $2,800. The $2,200 check was much more than my overtime would have made. This was only one of the many events in which God showed me His great desire to get His Gospel message into the hands of our troops. As of 2024, now-Master Sergeant Gabe Soileau is still helping to buy Bible literature for our troops through his retirement.

Not long after the conversation with the pastor who could not help me financially, God led me to contact a very old friend, Pastor Dale McCallister, at Maranatha Bible Church in Zanesville, Ohio. After I told him about my ministry, his church soon began to financially support the ministry with their missions program. Usually, this church sponsored a round-robin sort of missions conference of eight Bible-believing area churches; missionaries came for eight evening services and each night, a different missionary presented their work in one of the eight churches. Pastor McCallister invited me to present the work in the churches, and the church secretary later became our missions secretary, saving me quite a bit of time and work. Cindy, after 23 years is still with us. Her friendship and labor have been a tremendous help, encouragement, and joy to Judy and me. To this day, we still have churches supporting us from that round-robin missions conference.

For missionaries and other preachers, I want to insert a story about the importance of being willing to preach in a church, no matter the size. Preachers should preach to ten just like they would preach to a thousand. I had been praying for meetings to be scheduled where I could present the work. One day, I was praying as I headed to Michigan from Georgia. I had a Sunday open that could've been used as a travel day but I wanted to be in a church presenting the work for the troops. My friend at Maranatha Bible Church, Pastor Dale, gave me the phone number of a preacher in Ohio who might be interested in our mission. I called Sam's Creek Baptist Church, and the pastor made it clear that he had only eighteen folks in his Sunday morning congregation. I explained that I had been praying for a meeting and that God would use those eighteen people. He again explained that his small church could not help financially. Offering or not, I just wanted the church folks to know about the ministry. He allowed me to come to present the work.

After the service, the pastor said, "Brother Patrick, my son is the pastor of a Baptist church up the road. You need to call him for a meeting."

Sure enough, this church of about twenty-five folks allowed me to share my burden with them. So, I preached to them just like I would preach to a thousand. In the middle of the service, a man jumped up and ran out the back door. Having no idea of what caused this reaction, I continued preaching and then, after the service, began to pick up my ministry display materials. I knew many of our friends had been praying for the ministry, but I had not expected this result.

The man came back to the church and introduced himself by stating, "I have a friend down the street who is a brigadier general in the West Virginia National Guard. He is a chaplain and a pastor. I went to get him so he could meet you." This man who contacted his friend became a great supporter of the mission and is still helping us fifteen years later.

Chapter 16
Friendly Officers and a Giving Sergeant

Once we moved into the property in Jesup, Georgia, we still needed our own building to collate the packets. During these days of praying for a building, God continued to bless the street work. Often, police officers were very short and businesslike about our getting off the street. Once at Hulbert Air Force Base in Ft. Walton Beach, Florida, I was on the dirt median in the middle of the road, handing out Gospel tracts when a Florida highway patrol officer pulled up onto the island. When he exited his car, I knew people had been praying.

As he chared towards me, the first words out of his mouth to me were, "What in the world are you doing?"

I showed him the packet of Gospel literature and told him that we were sharing Bibles with the troops; he then said, "Praise the Lord! They need them."

He then asked, "Are you asking for money?"

Our answer was, "No, sir; we do not accept money on the streets."

He questioned me again: "Are you sure?" Then he said, "Keep up the good work, and do not get run over!"

Did conversations like this always happen? Absolutely not, but God knew when I needed encouragement and often sent Christian police officers to watch over us.

Not long after, PPG began laying off workers, and in 2005, it was my turn. But God showed up and made it clear Who was going to keep the mission moving forward. North Carolina state law requires that a company, when transferring a job to another country, retrain the employee for another job in the local area. This law, for me, sounded very nice, but I had been spending my time traveling to military bases and working the streets on my days off. I wasn't sure if I wanted to be retrained in another job or if I had the time. PPG laid me off.

I truly believe that God uses people just like He used the receptionist in Chicago to give me direction to pick up and move to Cambridge, Ohio, while I was sitting in Hammond. Before I was laid off from PPG, my co-worker Steve, a veteran who knew what I was doing on my days off, told me, "You need to take those Bibles you have to Savannah. Those Army Rangers need the Bible." His comments impressed me to drive to Savannah to check the streets to see if there was a gate where my type of evangelism would work. There was, and it was perfect.

Marty, another Army veteran at PPG, told me, "You need to go to Ft. Campbell Army Base in Clarksville, Tennessee." So I went.

Sure enough, the street in front of the main gate at Ft. Campbell had an island for me to stand on at a red-light intersection, causing the soldiers to stop. My first visit, four hundred miles away from my home in Lattimore, was interesting. During this time period, Muslims were handing out Islamic literature at the intersection down from me at the Savannah Hunter Army Airfield, and a group from the Westboro Baptist Church was protesting the war at the gate of Ft. Campbell in Hopkinsville, Kentucky, and here God sent me to both of these bases to encourage the troops with the packets of Gospel literature.

One day when I was at Ft. Campbell, after I had been there passing out literature, a police officer drove up to me and said, "Sir, you've been out here long enough; it's time for you to go home." His words were truly an answer to prayer – I needed that extra push to get back in my car and get some sleep before the long drive home. Marty, a man with no interest in the Gospel, was used by God to direct me to a base where troops truly needed some encouragement.

I need to backtrack in time to give some background about another police officer's reaction to my ministry. In 1978, I made the decision to attend Bible college in Hammond, Indiana. When my mother found out, she was part of a church that believed differently from the way that Judy and I believe the Bible teaches. Mother made it clear that she would pay for my college schooling if I would go to the college in Tulsa, Oklahoma. Paid schooling sounded great, but I knew the college in Tulsa did not line up with Scripture, and yet the college in Hammond did. Our decision to move to Hammond put a severe strain on the family relationship. I was pretty much no longer welcomed in my mother's house in Miami, where I grew up.

During the year 2008, my mother was in critical condition due to liver cancer. My wife and I drove to

Miami to see her, my brother, my sisters, and my step-siblings. When we arrived, we discovered that her attitude toward me had not changed but had also spread to my step-siblings. Because both of them had been on the other side of the law, they understood policemen and their power.

When I pulled out my Bible and began to read to comfort my mother at her bedside, my stepbrother told me to stop reading and leave or the police would be called. They called, and the police came. When I tried to defend myself, that this was the house that I grew up in for nineteen years, the police were not interested. One asked for my driver's license, and once he saw that I was a Georgia resident, I was ushered out to the front yard. Here, God showed up to encourage me during a pretty depressing time. Two more police showed up to remove me from the property – one went into the house to get a report from the first arriving officer while the other one stayed to guard me.

During some small talk, I asked the officer if I could go to my car to get a military packet created for soldiers. He agreed, and when I handed him the packet, he looked at me and said, "I'm retired out of Hunter Army Airfield in Savannah. There is some guy who stands in the incoming traffic handing these things out. I already have one. No, I'm not interested, but you have to leave the property, and these folks have requested a restraining order on you, so you cannot return to this property." Even in the middle of this discouraging event, God used this policeman to encourage me – God was already ahead of me! Little did I know while I was handing out packets in Savannah that one was handed to a man who would later cross paths with me in Miami!

Since being laid off from PPG in 2005, I had a choice to make: attend the school that the state suggested to be retrained for some other employment in North Carolina or keep up my street work, trusting the Lord that He would pay the bills. During one of the prayer times about the move to Georgia, my wife said, "If God is in this ministry, God will pay our bills."

Once the decision was made that I'd keep doing the street work, we knew something would have to happen about all the driving. From 2005 to 2019, we lived in Georgia, and I spent much time in the streets of Parris Island, Jacksonville Naval Base, and Hunter Army Airfield in Savannah, Georgia. The soldiers and Marines were very receptive to our type of evangelism – every morning during their physical training, the soldiers received a handwritten "Thank You for Our Freedom" note and a Gospel packet from a church.

Chapter 17
Federal Agents Stopped By

Hunter Army Airfield became a very good location for Gospel distribution. God continued to show a special interest in the military street work that He had established. One church in the Hinesville, Georgia, area offered to pay me to move to Hinesville, where Ft. Stewart and Hunter Army Airfield were located. We moved out of a double-wide mobile home with two acres of land into a mobile home park into a single-wide trailer with neighbors thirty feet away. My wife was a champion; she put up with so much baloney from me and is still supporting the mission all these years later.

We settled into nearby Ludowici and tried to work our mission in Hinesville, where Ft. Stewart was located, close to Hunter Army Airfield. We soon discovered that the police in the two cities, Hinesville and Savannah, had two different attitudes toward our mission work. I knew that the streets at Hunter Airfield, Parris Island Marine Corps Base, and Jacksonville Naval Base were all good locations for the street work. Once it was established that the streets in Hinesville were a "no-go," God gave me peace about my driving to the other three bases for early morning physical training (PT) traffic. This meant that I had to be up and on the road by 3:00 am if I were driving to Parris Island or Jacksonville Naval Base.

All these days, I never used an alarm clock. God used my time working at PPG (two twelve-hour days, then two twelve-hour nights) to adjust my body to waking at the appropriate times. During my factory days (1998-2005), the Lord trained me for a special mission - the streets and our soldiers! When I returned home from street work, my wife often asked me, "What time did you get up, and how did you get up without an alarm clock?" God blessed me. I know it was He Who woke me up to drive in the morning traffic at one of these three bases.

I didn't keep a diary of all the times God moved, but there were some times He moved that have not been forgotten. God had given me a young man to train to do the street work. One morning in Savannah at Hunter Army Airfield, we both received a wake-up call brought on by my using my camera.

All of this time that I was on the streets, I didn't realize that I was being watched so carefully until I had my young recruit take some pictures of me on the street in front of the gate. He might have had a half-dozen pictures in my camera when suddenly he had six federal agents surrounding him. They had him with his hands in the air, up against his car, and proceeded to confiscate my camera. We had always had good conversations while doing street work, but this morning, the conversation turned very serious, very quickly. We both prayed, and our Lord showed up with a few city police officers to help us out. The city police, most of whom were retired soldiers, knew what I had been doing in the streets. God used them to deliver the two of us from the federal agents. They acquired my camera, and we've never taken any more pictures of the front of a military base.

Chapter 18
A Police Officer and Gospel Dynamite

It was at Cherry Point Marine Corps Base that I learned a very valuable lesson on how to dress. Cherry Point, located on the Atlantic Ocean in North Carolina, was enjoying fall with a nice cool breeze that morning. I was at the red light in front of the gate. Everything was clicking. The Marines, most of the time, were very polite. That morning was no exception. I had on my Vietnam black leather jacket, black pants, and black boots. The local police showed up – a female officer not having a good morning and unfamiliar with us and our work. We assumed that she had been called to "check out the terrorist handing out dynamite." We had no dynamite, only Bibles.

"Raise your hands and walk over to me," were her first words. She had parked alongside the road and soon had me up against the car with my feet spread and hands up against the car. Within minutes, her backup came – a retired Marine police officer who got my hands down and started to talk with me like a gentleman. During the next few minutes, he had a nice talk with the other officer, who got in her squad car and pulled out. Someone was definitely praying for us!

Now, the Marine police officer said to me, "Let's take a look at your car." That was a good morning for my car. He opened all the doors.

When he saw the boxes of literature in the back seat, he said, "Let's take a look in your trunk." In a move that only God could orchestrate, he had me open the trunk, which was lined with boxes full of packets – hundreds of packets for our troops. Praise the Lord! They were all nice and in order.

He looked at me and said, "You gotta be a Baptist."

He shut the trunk, and we chatted for a few minutes about his church and the street. However, I was on federal property, and thus, I had to leave. But it was a good morning for our Savior—a few hundred "little preachers" (aka Gospel tracts) were sent into Cherry Point, and the police officer drove away praising the Lord.

Our collating of the packets became a real challenge. We were in our first church in South Georgia, trying to get help with the collating process, when God allowed my path to cross with several new pastors in Georgia and Michigan who are still helping with this ministry.

In 2008, in Michigan, I met Pastor Adam Summers, who had a tremendous desire to teach his church the importance of world missions. The distance between this Michigan pastor and our mission in Georgia was no problem; we both had the vision to glorify our Lord through the tract distribution in the streets. God raised up a godly man who loved driving – Scott Petrie. Only God could've allowed our paths to cross. One day, I needed help to pick up a load of Gospel literature in Georgia to be collated in Michigan. Scott was eager to help and did so that time and many other times!

It was in 2009 that we started teaching Faith Baptist Church in Chelsea, Michigan, how God had led us to collate our military packets. That first summer, we had collated about 10,000 packets. One day, I was preparing to leave Chelsea – the motor coach was loaded, the doors were locked - and Scott Petrie, a dog salesman, approached me about buying a dog to take on our journeys. Once I convinced him that I did not need a dog, he handed an envelope to me. After I noticed the picture of a dog on it, I noticed the ten $100 bills inside. Scott had just sold a dog for $1,000 and gave me the dog money. So, in a way, I guess I did get a dog. Scott's death a few years later of a respiratory disease was a major loss to our mission and to me personally. Scott was a dear friend.

Chapter 19
Cancer and the Furtherance of the Gospel

During the mission work in Georgia, prostate cancer showed its ugly head. The doctor at the VA hospital in Charleston, South Carolina, wanted to remove the prostate surgically. This was a matter of serious prayer about what type of procedure I should have to remove the cancer. We heard about the cancer center at the VA hospital in Ann Arbor, Michigan, close to Willis, Michigan, where we had previously visited a church for support meetings. The Lord was ahead of me, as usual. He touched the heart of an RV park owner who allowed us to park our fifth wheel on his property for free for the three months of surgery and chemo.

This time of cancer treatments at the hospital was a tremendous opportunity to share the Gospel packets with sick veterans. We were also able to find new churches in Michigan who were interested in the mission, and to this day, we have churches that still help us due to our visit there.

Once I was finished with the cancer treatment, we decided to try to get more church members involved in the ministry - adults in writing personal thank you cards and children in coloring pictures – for us to include in the packets. This coloring of picture sheets started at White Plains Christian School in Mt. Airy, North Carolina. I had finished preaching when the principal, David Tucker, approached me with some coloring sheets from some of his students and asked me if I could use them in our packets. That day, God started a part of the ministry that has been a blessing to many children . . . and to senior citizens. I discovered that many senior citizens, especially those in nursing homes, use coloring as a therapeutic tool. The original ministry of handing out copies of John and Romans has now gone into Christian schools and senior citizen homes. Thousands of folks have been helped by that part of our mission.

The miles continued to stretch out before us, and God continued to provide the means for the miles.

I started on the road with a one-ton van and a former FEMA trailer – my introduction to the travel trailer industry. It was not long until I found myself in the hospital from breathing formaldehyde that was enclosed in that trailer. Once we solved the formaldehyde problem, God provided the means to buy a Ford 350 diesel dual-wheel truck and a fifth-wheel trailer. The equipment would have been great if I were a retiree and wanted to travel from campground to campground. However, I was not using the equipment for the right purpose (we constantly had it heavily loaded with Bible literature), and thus, the truck and trailer did not last very long.

Once we were able to sell the fifth-wheel trailer, God provided us with a twenty-eight-foot bumper-pulled trailer. My wife Judy and I lived in it for a number of years while traveling to the bases and new churches. Soon, I turned that twenty-eight-foot trailer into a freight truck and trailer, and again, the trailer didn't last long. God graciously provided a thirty-eight-foot Holiday

Rambler motor coach, and we purchased a Toyota Prius electric car. We bought a box trailer to carry more literature and the Prius since it could not be pulled behind the coach. We drove these vehicles from Georgia, to military bases in California, to the Dakotas, and to Michigan.

Chapter 20
A Stroke and Some "Good News"

In 2015, God had another evangelistic tool prepared for Berean Armed Forces Ministries (BAFM). I had been buying pocket-sized copies of John and Romans from my good friend Evangelist Dennis Deneau in Lansing, Michigan. One day, before I left his warehouse, he introduced me to the Good News John and Romans newspaper – the book of John and the book of Romans printed in newspaper form. God knew my 2019 stroke was coming and that I'd be off the streets passing out literature so He had a bigger idea than even Dennis Deneau had. In 2015, I was still pretty healthy, and I thought I would just install the Good News newspaper anywhere a store manager would allow me to.

This was an answer to prayer. Pretty soon, God was using Berean Armed Forces Ministries to print His Word and pay local newspaper companies to deliver the Good News to the homes of the subscribers to the local newspapers. Before we even asked, God had prepared the way for the John and Romans to be delivered to homes of military folk near MacDill Air Force Base, Ft. Stewart Army Base, Shaw Air Force Base, Warner Robbins Air Force Base, and Ft. Campbell Army Base in Hopkinsville, Kentucky. No more standing in the street and speaking to 200-250 drivers, one car at a time, in the morning traffic. Now, we have 5,000-10,000 Good News newspapers being delivered by the local newspaper companies. God is always ahead of us.

Once when I was buying fuel in Walterboro, South Carolina, at a Burger King/Exxon station, I walked into the grocery area to see if they had a magazine rack in which I could put the Good News. Behind the counter were a father and son who practiced the Hindu religion. When I introduced myself and my request of distributing the Good News, the young cashier said, "Sir, put your paper right here, and maybe some of these people will pick it up and read it and believe what it says and then stop stealing from me!" He simply recognized the power of the Good News!

This Good News newspaper has been a great evangelistic tool! People from all around the US have called me, asking questions about what they read.

In 2019, God began to show me His plan for our Good News John and Romans. As I was loading the trailer to move from Jesup, Georgia, back to Shelby, North Carolina, with thousands of copies of John and Romans, our military packets, and all our office equipment, I suffered my first stroke. And yet, God showed His mercy and patience with me. I was at the property by myself, the office building was all locked up, and I was not feeling well at all. I managed to get back behind the wheel of the motor coach (the 38-foot Holiday Rambler, the twenty-eight-foot trailer loaded with literature and the Prius), and God allowed me to drive my rig heading toward the Charleston VA hospital. I'm not sure how many guardian angels were used on me that day, but I did not complete the three-hour drive.

God allowed me to reach Walterboro, South Carolina, to the property of the pastor of Welch Creek

Baptist Church, James Baker. His wife, a previous nurse, was pretty sure I had had a stroke. Since my rig was safe on their property, the Bakers contacted Judy, who drove from Shelby, North Carolina, to take me to the VA hospital in Charleston, South Carolina, where I stayed for about two weeks and had many opportunities to give the Gospel with the veterans there.

Soon, the hospital transported me to a Charlotte, North Carolina, rehabilitation hospital closer to my home in Shelby, where I had physical therapy and care for about a month. Here, God spoke through a medical doctor to help me see that my ministry was not over. When he finished the paperwork to discharge me, he said these words, "Patrick, you have two choices in life: you can go home and become a couch potato, or you can go back to your mission. I hope and pray that you will go back to your mission. America needs what you have been doing."

That statement has been in my head ever since: "America needs what you have been doing."

Chapter 21
Little is Much with God

In the summer of 2019, God again showed me the importance of this Good News newspaper of John and Romans. Judy's Aunt Betty, living in Maggie Valley, Tennessee, fell and broke her hip. This news required a trip to Aunt Betty's home, some 110 miles from our home in Fallston, North Carolina. This trip showed Judy and me that God could use a ten-cent newspaper – as we distributed it in the Huddle House restaurant, Ingles grocery store, and multiple gas stations. Judy always knew that a two-hour trip (like one hundred ten miles to see Aunt Betty) would turn into a three- or four-hour trip since we stopped quite a bit to distribute the newspaper. Judy was probably ready for the extra time, but we were not ready for what God was preparing to show us.

It was at a BI-LO grocery store in Maggie Valley that God showed Himself real to me again. BI-LO had always allowed the Good News newspaper to be installed in their paper racks, so I was not expecting any problem installing the paper at this location. Whenever I meet a store manager to ask permission to install the paper, I always use the military packet of Gospel literature to explain my ministry. On this particular day, I saw a young adult with a group of teenagers at a cash register; it looked as if the adult was giving instructions on operating the cash register. I assumed that the adult was the store manager, so I waited for him to finish his instructions.

Folks pray constantly for this ministry of Gospel literature distribution, and I wish those prayer warriors had been present that day to see God answer their prayers. God works in mysterious ways, always on time.

When the man finished his instructions, I approached him and addressed him as the store manager. I began my introduction with a military packet, explained my ministry, and asked him for permission to install the Good News newspaper in his store. The man let me run through my whole presentation.

Then he said, "I'm not the store manager." My heart didn't really want to hear that, but then he continued talking.

"I am the Command Sergeant Major of the North Carolina Army Guard. I'm here working with these Maggie Valley teenagers, giving them instructions on working in public. Now, Sir, I want you to take that military packet to our headquarters in Raleigh, North Carolina, and tell the chaplain that I sent you and that all our Army Guard needs this packet."

I took this turn of events as from God – I was trying to install the Good News in just one grocery store, and God wanted it in the Army Guard headquarters 280 miles east of where I was. However, this task was not simple. I had Judy with me, and we were on the way to check on her Aunt Betty. I cannot remember all the specific timing of this event, but as I got out of the way during the next few months, 2,400 Gospel packets were placed into the hands of North Carolina guardsmen and their families. Here's the story:

Once I returned Judy to our home, I loaded the car and headed for the Army Guard Armory, and it just seemed as if God were leading the whole trip. I'm sure that most Americans have a cell phone with mapping capability, but I got my directions to Raleigh another way… after I got lost. Once I realized that fact, I started looking for a gas station to get directions. At 5 am, God led me to a 7-Eleven convenience store. I was bracing myself to speak to someone who had a very strong accent and who probably didn't know the way to the Army Armory. I was right, but God had another plan. When I entered the store, only one other customer was present getting a cup of coffee. I followed the man out of the store and caught up with him before he got to his car. Thinking that I was a beggar, he told me that he couldn't help me. I introduced myself and asked if he knew where the Army Guard Armory was located.

As soon as I asked that question, the words he then spoke instantly told me that God was in absolute control. He looked me over and asked me my reason for going to the Armory. With this open door to explain the military packets I had with me, I shared with him the Command Sergeant Major's order that I bring them to the chaplain.

This man, whom I had seemingly met at random, explained that he was a police officer with a New Jersey force and that he was currently assigned to the North Carolina Army Guard. Then he said, "Get in your car and follow me. I will take you to the chaplain."

Oh, you should've been there to see God pave the way for the distribution of His Word. The guardsman spoke the right words to get me into the Armory parking lot; then he pushed all the right numbers into the entrance doors to get me into the building, and then he led me straight to the chaplain. While waiting at the chaplain's office for him to show up, I knew God had sent this guardsman to bring me exactly where I had been authorized to go by the Command Sergeant Major in Maggie Valley... and by the Commander of the Universe, my Heavenly Father, Who does all things well.

I explained to the chaplain what had happened in Maggie Valley. He let me know that he had seen the packets before and spoke highly of the material. He then told me that he would have to have the approval of his command before he could allow me to distribute them. The next words from his mouth made me realize the importance of the distribution of the Good News newspapers at the Maggie Valley BI-LO store. He asked, "How many of these do you have with you? We have 2,000 troops from North Carolina deploying to Kuwait during the next few months."

During those next few months, deployment briefings were held at various large conference areas that could hold hundreds of soldiers, and we had permission to attend with our Gospel packets. And that's how 2,400 Gospel packets were placed in the hands of soldiers and their family members who attended the briefings. All this just because of Aunt Betty's broken hip and our trying to install the Good News at the Maggie Valley BI-LO!

Now, here is another blessing. During this time of working with the deployment briefings – passing out Gospel packets – our ministry, Berean Armed Forces

Ministry, didn't pay one dime for our housing and food. Judy and I were allowed to stay at hotels and eat at restaurants at the expense of the military budget.

If you are a Gospel seed sower, keep planting the seed everywhere God leads you, for He has a plan for every seed planted.

Chapter 22
The American Legion

Also, in 2019, just after my stroke, the American Legion was celebrating its 100th anniversary in Indianapolis, Indiana. I failed to realize that a pass must be obtained to enter the convention center gate, and then a ticket must be purchased to enter the convention hall itself. When I arrived, I carried all my packets and my table from the parking garage to the entrance gate about half a mile - only to be told that a pass was required. I stood there, the gate guarded by police, when God began to pave my way. A police officer who had nothing to do with the American Legion noticed what I had in my suitcases – Gospel packets – and told the guard, an American legionnaire – to let me enter. I know God had sent this man for I had no pass, and I paid no entrance fee.

It was just a few months after that convention when God moved His Word again. I received a phone call from an American legionnaire in Corinth, Mississippi, "Sir, are you the man who makes the Devoted Service packets with all the Gospel literature in there? We have a tremendous problem with suicide here in Mississippi. My mother brought home one of these from Indianapolis, and we could use about two thousand of them. Can you help us?"

Our trip to the Indiana convention led to these two thousand packets being delivered to Mississippi to nursing homes, hospitals, and individual American Legion Posts throughout the state. That one trip also led to a meeting with the head of the Mississippi National Guard Family Resource Center, who now uses our materials in their care boxes that are shipped to individual soldiers deployed to combat zones across the world. The American Legion still allows us to attend their conventions and share the Gospel packets. God definitely leads, one step at a time.

Four years later, we're still reaping the fruit from that Mississippi contact. Here's a message from a friend of the ministry that came in December 2023: "It's great to hear from you. Sorry, I haven't let C. or you know when and where I've sent the [1700] packets. I sent all those you brought earlier last year; some to Poland, Egypt, South Korea, on a boat in the Persian Gulf, and Kuwait… about 400 to Kuwait in December. We have some new units that left recently that we will send most of these others [with]." "Little preachers" are literally all the way around the world because we followed the Lord's call to be at the celebration of the 100th year of the American Legion! Only God could do this!

Chapter 23
God's Timing and a Storm at Golden Corral

So much could be written about the day we prayed about the opportunity to share the Gospel packets at the Golden Corral in Ft. Walton Beach, Florida. God had allowed me to see the long lines on Veteran's Day in 2012. Now, as the veterans come to the restaurant for their free meal, Berean Armed Forces Ministry is there alongside local church members to hand a packet to each veteran and family member and to shake their hand, telling them "Thank you" for their service to America. This opportunity allows so many of God's children to witness in public, telling others about Him. Since that first Golden Corral, God blessed us in 2019, allowing us to present the packets in forty-nine restaurants. Then came 2020 and Covid-19 hit, and the numbers declined.

In October 2021, North Carolina was expecting a tropical storm which included some pretty severe wind and rain. The Lord impressed me to drive to Jacksonville, North Carolina, where Marine Corps Camp Lejeune is located near a Golden Corral. I was questioning myself while I was driving to see about setting up our table to hand out packets to the veterans on Veteran's Day. I have driven in all kinds of weather, but for some reason, this wind was different. When I entered the Golden Corral, I found out why God had sent me in a tremendous rainstorm. I mentioned to the cashier that I was with a military mission, and she immediately moved to find the manager, who came over to introduce himself. I explained my reason for being there, and he said, "Sir, this is your lucky day. The owner of the restaurant is here today."

I definitely do not believe in luck, for God is in control. It seems that, because of the heavy rain and wind, the owner didn't want to leave, so he was there for me to meet. The owner approached me, introduced himself, and offered for me to come eat with him. Is this not God working?!? We ate and discussed our life stories: he had been working in Golden Corral ever since he was a kid. His dad had borrowed money from the bank to start the first ever Golden Corral, put him to work in the kitchen, and then sent him to college. This owner had owned twenty-five Golden Corrals until Covid hit when he lost thirteen.

Then, I brought out the military packet. He moved his plate over and carefully opened the packet, looking attentively at each tract. He then told me, "I have twelve restaurants, and I want this material at all of them."

I had too small of a goal – I had wanted only one restaurant and now God was giving me twelve restaurants! God continues to open doors for us to spread His message of salvation.

These Veteran's Day events include multiple churches sharing the packets with numerous veterans from Ft. Lauderdale, Florida, to Syracuse, New York, to Austin, Texas, and we had been given permission to visit more than thirty restaurants, which include seven different restaurant chains to share the Gospel.

A Final Story

One more story about the power of God moving His Word. December 23, 2023, I was in an Ollie's grocery store and was standing behind a mother and daughter in a long line. Eventually, the mother let her stress over the season ruin her attitude so she left her credit card for the daughter to pay for the groceries and went to sit in her car. The daughter turned and saw my Vietnam hat. She spoke very quietly, "Thank you for my freedom." Her comment opened the door for me to speak openly with her, so I pulled a tract out and handed it to her, explaining that I had written the tracts for the soldiers over at Ft. Bragg. She looked stunned and then explained, "That's where we're from. My dad works at Ft. Bragg." She put the tract in her pocket as the cashier began to scan her items.

Here, in Shelby, 225 miles away from Ft. Bragg, I met a girl whose father is stationed at Ft. Bragg. I will probably never see her again, but God's Word, in the form of a "Little Preacher," a Gospel tract, will go with her, offering her the true plan of salvation.

Before 9/11, God had impressed me with Acts 10 which tells about the life of an army captain of the Italian band, Cornelius. This chapter in Acts helps drive me to do what I'm doing for the Lord and for our armed forces. Much was accomplished for God because of Cornelius' simple obedience. You've read about a soldier - me - who was doing good deeds for our Lord yet was unsaved. God used some very unusual tactics to get the Gospel message to the soldier. Please know that all you've read was done by God.

All these opportunities are really answers to prayer from Christians who want the plan of salvation to be spread. From the brown Florsheim Imperial shoes that I had asked God for to the opening of so many restaurant chains where hundreds of Christian volunteers can work for Him, we are so blessed.

As you can see from the stories in this book, God answers prayer – He actually listens in love and in power. I hope and pray that talking to God will be part of your daily routine, from the "good morning" to God to the "good night" to God. Grab a notebook and begin to record those times when you and God are talking quietly to each other. Start seeing what God wants to do for you. You will be amazed.

Epilogue

Berean Armed Forces Ministries has no rich donors other than our Almighty God, Who patiently and lovingly has constantly paid the bills for this ministry to spread His Word. The only reason I can understand that He would do so is found in Psalm 138:1-2: "I will praise thee with my whole heart: before the gods will I sing praise unto thee. I will worship toward thy holy temple and praise thy name for thy lovingkindness and for thy truth: for thou hast magnified thy word above all thy name."

I have known that I could never worship God from a public pulpit with my singing or with a stringed instrument. So, I asked God to show me a pure way in which I would be able to worship Him Sunday to Sunday. This passage was my answer—my magnifying His Word by giving it to the lost is the way He wants me to praise Him.

Most Christians have available to them the very Word of God in the form of "little preachers" (Gospel tracts). Giving out copies of God's Word is a simple yet effective way to worship our God "before the gods" of this world. Could it be that the financial success of Berean Armed Forces Ministries is due to God's seeing these "little preachers" being given and He still wants them to continue going out?

In summary of this work from 2001 to 2024, ponder these numbers: 290,000 Gospel packets, all paid for, holding twenty "little preachers," equal 5,800,000 tracts, also paid for. These tracts were not given to the ministry for free. God, through His people, paid for everything we've done and continues to pave the financial way. God is not ashamed to pay for His work.

God's people, from elementary school age to the elderly in assisted living homes, have thrown their energy into coloring pictures and handwriting "thank you" notes for these packets.

When we moved out of Indiana to Ohio to start a church in 1985, a friend told me, "Patrick, there is a fine line between faith and foolishness, and it sounds as if what you're doing is very foolish." Evidently, God thinks otherwise. Some men at my age of seventy-four years have many investments bringing in money for their retirement; however, I believe that God has allowed me to miss those investment opportunities so that I would rely on Him and His people for His work. How can this be foolish when God is in it?!

Throughout the years of this ministry, God has graciously given us a van, a FEMA trailer, a Ford 350 diesel 3-seater, a one-ton dual-wheel pick-up truck, a fifth-wheel trailer, a thirty-eight-foot Holiday Rambler motor coach, and a twenty-six-foot box trailer. After selling the motor coach, we purchased a fifty-five-foot sea container and a 40 x 12 storage building for our materials.

I'm hoping that you've learned the one main lesson from this book: God will provide to have His Word published and to have His Name exalted among the gods of this world.

If you'd like to have a part in this ministry, please send your contribution to BAFM, 2400 Chandlersville Road, Zanesville, Ohio, 43701.

Made in the USA
Columbia, SC
16 September 2024